Cursive
HANDWRITING
WORKBOOK

ALPHABET, JOKES, FUNNY PHRASES AND MORE!

over 157 pages full of funny jokes and riddles for KIDS!

Copyright © Cursive Hand
P U B L I S H I N G

Cursive Handwriting Workbook
Alphabet, Jokes, Funny Phrases and More!
Copyright © Cursive Handwriting Publishing

Hello Future
Cursive Handwriting
Master!

We firmly believe that the art and skill of cursive writing is both beautiful and important. We live in the digital age, but the most beautiful and important words are still written by hand.

There are many benefits to having cursive writing skills. Writing in cursive you don't just form words more easily, you also write better sentences. It's proven that kids who learned and wrote in cursive experienced an increase in skills related to syntax.

Cursive will also help you develop your unique signature. As an adult, you will need to sign important documents - a handwritten signature is much more difficult to forge! What's more, writing in cursive is faster than writing in type, and this skill is incredibly practical and helpful especially when studying and test taking scenarios. And we don't think you will deny that a handwritten letter is much more valuable and romantic than one that is printed or sent by e-mail!

It is also well known that play is the highest form of learning! That's why this workbook will guide you from the very beginning - from learning how to write single letters, to joins and short words to writing whole sentences - in a fun and entertaining way.

Instead of rewriting boring sentences, you will practice on jokes! Instead of getting bored writing the same thing over and over again, you'll be copying and making up your own funny sentences. And as a break, you can play cryptogram and word search! Sounds good, doesn't it?

So practice, copy, create,
write, and remember to always
have fun!

One very important thing you need to know at the beginning is that there is not one and only one correct way to write in cursive. Most adults have developed their own style of writing, which has been established over many years. It is usually cobbled together from printing and cursive techniques.

In schools, one form of cursive is usually chosen and taught, and most often it's one of four common cursive handwriting types: **New American Cursive, Handwriting Without Tears, D'Nealian and Zaner-Bloser.**

So it may happen that someone older than you looks at this workbook and says: „Oh no! I learned differently! I write G completely differently! There are mistakes here!" v.

But nothing more wrong!

Just look at the examples of how the same letters can be written differently and each way is correct:

There are different methods, and while the spelling of individual letters may vary from time to time, they are all about the same thing - to teach you to write fluently and effortlessly. If you do all the exercises in this notebook correctly, your handwriting will noticeably improve, become more aesthetic and you will really enjoy it!

Over time, as you write more often, you will develop your own style, which may be slightly different from the one we want to teach you now. But our goal is not to teach you the only correct writing style, but to give you the basics, make you like handwriting and use this skill every day with pleasure and satisfaction. That's what we want! And you want it too, since you're holding this workbook in your hands!

For some letters, you will have the opportunity to practice spelling the two versions. Choose the version that suits you best, looks better, or is more comfortable for you to write, and practice this version in the following exercises. If you need help, you can ask someone more experienced to add the chosen version of the letter to the exercises. In the meantime, get to know the whole alphabet that is waiting for you and get to work!

Aa Bb Cc Dd Ee
Ff Gg Hh Ii Jj
Kk Ll Mm Nn
Oo Pp Qq Rr Ss
Tt Uu Vv Ww
Xx Yy Zz

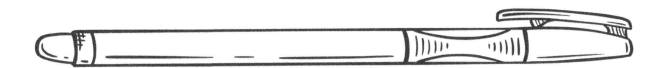

And here's what you'll find inside:

For each letter of the alphabet there are 6 pages full of interesting and entertaining exercises:

1. Single letter practice!

2. Joining letters!

3. Writing short words!

4. Copying funny sentences!

5. Funny cryptogram puzzles!

6. Tracing funny jokes!

7. Coming up with hilarious sentences!

8. Extra page with creative writing prompt and space for drawing funny illustration!

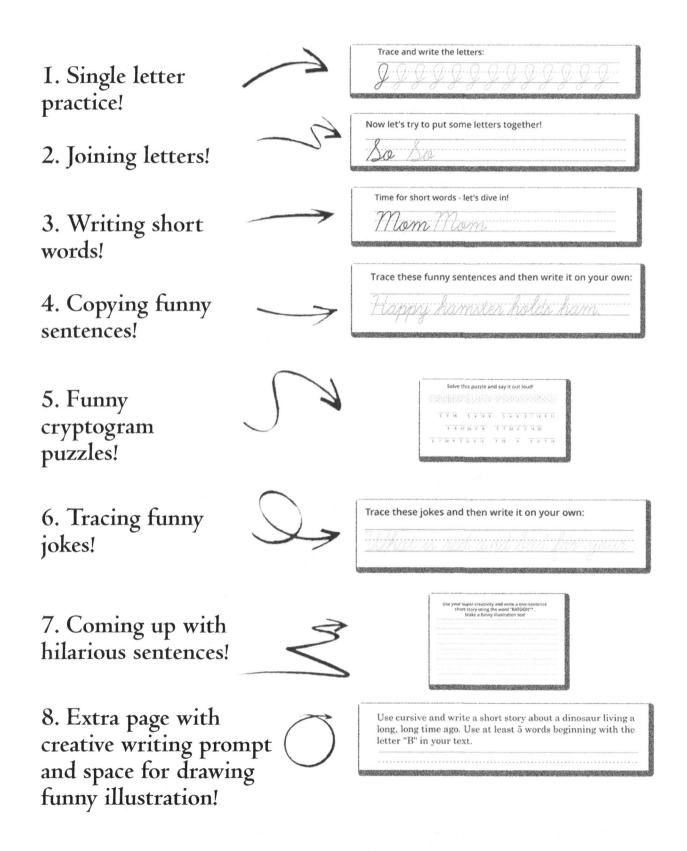

Some *tips*
to help you start:

Above all, always remember to sit comfortably when writing. Place your feet flat on the floor, straighten your back, relax your shoulders - good posture is essential.

If you're using a pencil, choose a pencil with a soft B tip. If you prefer something else, a felt-tip pen or gel pen is best, as it has fluid delivery of ink and allows you to write smoothly.

Don't limit your exercises to paper only! Be creative, draw letters in the air, in the sand, on your friend's back - let them guess what you wrote! Make it fun and creative!

Remember to hold the pencil correctly. It is important that the tip of the thumb connects with the pencil. Only the correct grip will guarantee that in the future you will write quickly and fluently.

Each letter has up to eight pages of exercises and each subsequent one is more difficult. Therefore, if you are just starting to learn cursive handwriting, we suggest first doing the first exercise for each letter, then the second one, and so on. It will be easier for you to write letter connections fo you practice writing each letter separately first, just as it will be to write short words if you practice connecting each letter to the others beforehand. Good luck, future

Master of Cursive Handwriting

Currently, there are 65 different alphabets used worldwide. The richest of them is Khmer, which has 72 letters, while the most economical is the alphabet of one of the languages of Papua New Guinea, which requires only 11 letters.

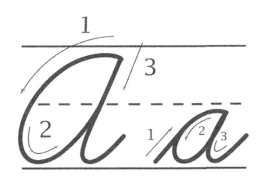

Trace and write the letters:

$\mathcal{A}$ a a a a a a a a a a a a a a

$\mathcal{A}$ a a

$\mathcal{A}$

a a a a a a a a a a a a a a a a a a

a a a

a

Now let's try to put some letters together!

$\mathcal{A}n$ $\mathcal{A}n$ $\mathcal{A}n$

$\mathcal{A}i$ $\mathcal{A}i$ $\mathcal{A}i$

$\mathcal{A}s$ $\mathcal{A}s$ $\mathcal{A}s$

am *am* *am*

ac *ac* *ac*

ai *ai* *ai*

as *as* *as*

Time for short words - let's dive in!

And *And* *And*

Arm *Arm* *Arm*

App *App* *App*

ape *ape* *ape*

ant *ant* *ant*

ace *ace* *ace*

aid *aid* *aid*

I was with my grandpa at the museum and because I had practiced cursive beforehand, I could read the map to find the hidden treasure! It was so freaking awesome! (Adam, age 8)

The uppercase letter „A" can be also written in this way:

A A A A A

A

A

An An An

Ai Ai Ai

As As As

Ar Ar Ar

Al Al Al

Ac Ac Ac

Ak Ak Ak

And another version of short words:

And *And And*

Arm *Arm Arm*

Axe *Axe Axe*

App *App App*

Ape *Ape Ape*

Ant *Ant Ant*

Ace *Ace Ace*

Ash *Ash Ash*

Amp *Amp Amp*

Aid *Aid Aid*

China produces 38 billion pens every year - enough to give each person on Earth over 5 pens (80% of the world's pen production). Despite such enormous production, until recently, Chinese companies had to import pen tips from abroad because they did not have the technology to produce parts with sufficient precision.

Trace these funny sentences and then write them on your own!

All adventorous animals
admire artistic apples.

All adventorous animals
admire artistic apples.

Angry amber ants agitate
against avid anteaters.

Angry amber ants agitate
against avid anteaters.

Trace these jokes and then write them on your own:

What one plate says to the other? Dinner is on me!

What one

Why did the cookie go to the doctor? Because it felt crumbly.

Why did

The largest writing pen in the world was built in India. It is 5.5 meters long and weighs 37 kilograms. The smallest pen is the „Nanofountain Probe", which is used for writing on chips in nanoscale. The line created by this pen is 40 nanometers wide. Also the Ohto Minimo is very small and is measuring only 91 mm in length and 3.7 mm in width!

Use your super creativity and write a one-sentence short story using the word „ABECEDARIAN"*.

----

*ABECEDARIAN is anyone who is currently learning the alphabet, so basically all preschoolers, for example.

Solve this puzzle and say it out loud!

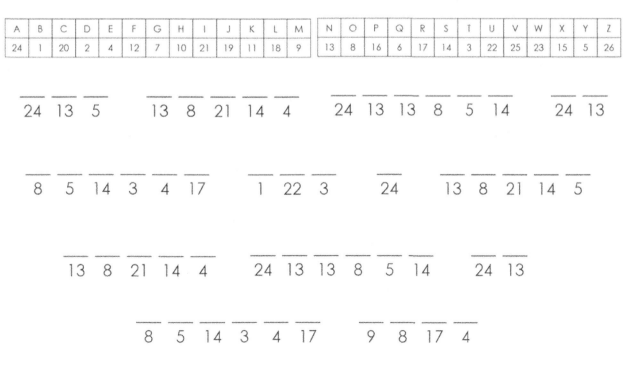

Extra page in case you want to practice some more!

Use cursive and write what you would like to invent? Use at least 5 words beginning with the letter „A" in your text...

...and draw a funny illustration!

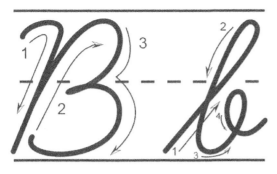

Trace and write the letters:

B B B B B B B B B B B B B

B B B

B

b b b b b b b b b b b b b b b

b b b

b

Now let's try to put some letters together!

Be Be Be

Bi Bi Bi

Br Br Br

The lowercase letter „b" can also be written in this way:

b b b b b b b b b b

b b b b b b b b b b

b b b b b b b b b b

b b b

b

bl bl bl

bn bn bn

bs bs bs

bc bc bc

bk bk bk

br br br

be be be

Or like this:

b b b b b b b b b b

b b b b b b b b b b

b b b b b b b b b b

b b b

b

bl bl bl

bn bn bn

bs bs bs

bc bc bc

bk bk bk

br br br

be be be

ba *ba ba*

bc *bc bc*

bi *bi bi*

bn *bn bn*

Time for short words – let's dive in!

Big *Big Big*

Bill *Bill Bill*

Bit *Bit Bit*

ball *ball ball*

bat *bat bat*

boy *boy boy*

box *box box*

Trace these funny sentences and then write them on your own!

Beloved babies bravely

babble before bedtime.

Beautiful birds business is

beating brown bugs.

Trace these jokes and then write them on your own:

What do you say to a frog who needs a ride? "Hop in."

What do

What do we call a dinosaur can crash? Tyrannosaurus wrecks.

What do

The history of the fountain pen is quite mysterious. The first mention of a pen with ink in a reservoir dates back to the second half of the 10th century in North Africa, where a certain Maad al-Muizz demanded a pen that would not dirty his hands. The next mention comes only from the 16th century - from the German inventor Daniel Schwenter.

Use your super creativity and write a one-sentence short story using the word „BUMFUZZLE"*.

*BUMFUZZLED is an adjective and means a state of bewilderment - to be dazed or confused.

Solve this puzzle and say it out loud!

A	B	C	D	E	F	G	H	I	J	K	L	M
18	13	3	8	2	22	26	25	4	5	21	6	1

N	O	P	Q	R	S	T	U	V	W	X	Y	Z
11	12	15	9	23	19	24	10	17	7	16	20	14

13 2 24 24 20   13 12 24 24 2 23   13 12 10 26 25 24

19 12 1 2   13 10 24 24 2 23   13 10 24

19 25 2   19 18 4 8   24 25 2

13 10 24 24 2 23 19   13 4 24 24 2 23

Extra page in case you want to practice some more!

Use cursive and write a short story about dinosaur living a long, long time ago. Use at least 5 words beginning with the letter „B" in your text...

...and draw a funny illustration!

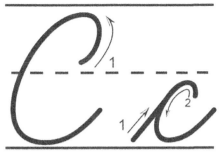 

Trace and write the letters:

C C C C C C C C C C C C C C C

C C C C

C

c c c c c c c c c c c c c c c c

c c c c

c

Now let's try to put some letters together!

Cu Cu Cu

Ci Ci Ci

Cy Cy Cy

ce   ce   ce

cd   cd   cd

cj   cj   cj

ca   ca   ca

Time for short words - let's dive in!

Can   Can   Can

Cake   Cake   Cake

Cell   Cell   Cell

cat   cat   cat

cow   cow   cow

cup   cup   cup

cot   cot   cot

I read in one book that children who wrote by hand activated the area of the brain used for reading. So when I practice writing, the part of my brain that I use to read is also developing! It's great because I love reading and I want to get better at it! (Jonathan, age 9)

Trace these funny sentences and then write them on your own!

Crazy clowns cook crazy
crispy coconut cupcakes.

Crazy clowns cook crazy
crispy coconut cupcakes.

Creative cozy call center
chef chews colorful carrots.

Creative cozy call center
chef chews colorful carrots.

Trace these jokes and then write them on your own:

What kind of car does Yoda drive? A toyoda!

What

What do you call a Ford Fiesta that ran out of gas? A Ford Siesta.

What do

With a bit of imagination, you can use an ordinary pen (such as a Bic) to... lure termites out of the house. This is because some inks used in pens emit a scent identical to the pheromones that termites use to mark paths leading to food. When hungry, termites can just easily follow a path drawn with a pen by mistake.

Use your super creativity and write a one-sentence short story using the word „CATTYWAMPUS"*.

*CATTYWAMPUS means askew, awry, kitty-corner. This word is a variant of catawampus, another example of great American slang from the 19th century. It can also mean „an imaginary fierce wild animal" or „savage, destructive".

Solve this puzzle and say it out loud!

A	B	C	D	E	F	G	H	I	J	K	L	M
18	12	6	23	22	20	4	17	1	10	15	7	9

N	O	P	Q	R	S	T	U	V	W	X	Y	Z
16	26	24	3	2	25	8	19	13	14	11	5	21

6 18 16   5 26 19   6 18 16   18   6 18 16

18 25   18   6 18 16 16 22 2   6 18 16

6 18 16   18   6 18 16

Extra page in case you want to practice some more!

Use cursive and write where you would go if you could time travel.
Use at least 5 words beginning with the letter „C" in your text...

...and draw a funny illustration!

Trace and write the letters:

Now let's try to put some letters together!

dn dn dn

dj dj dj

dl dl dl

dh dh dh

Time for short words - let's dive in!

Dice Dice Dice

Den Den Den

Deer Deer Deer

dig dig dig

dog dog dog

dad dad dad

duck duck duck

When I visited my grandmother in the nursing home, I could read her old letters and diaries written in cursive. It was amazing, I felt like I was traveling back in time and got to know my grandma so much better! (Eve, age 11)

Trace these funny sentences and then write them on your own!

Dumb dutiful deer dated a divine dapper doberman.

Dumb dutiful deer dated a divine dapper doberman.

Determined daddy did delightful dandy dances.

Determined daddy did delightful dandy dances.

Trace these jokes and then write them on your own:

What do you call a unicorn
with no horn? A horse.

What do

Why couldn't the frog
find where he parked his
car? He'd been toad.

Why

Handwriting is never the same for two people, even for twins! Just like fingerprints and palm lines are unique, handwriting is also one-of-a-kind!

Use your super creativity and write a one-sentence short story using the word „DOLLOP"*.

_____

- -

_____

- -

_____

- -

_____

- -

_____

- -

*DOLLOP is a small, indefinite amount of something. You can ask for a dollop of sour cream on the taco or have great dollops of cream. This is an example of a word meaning the amount of something that is not exact.

Solve this puzzle and say it out loud!

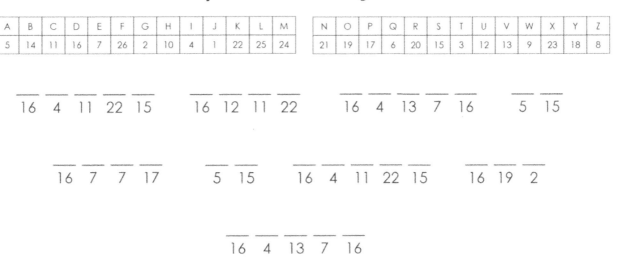

A	B	C	D	E	F	G	H	I	J	K	L	M
5	14	11	16	7	26	2	10	4	1	22	25	24

N	O	P	Q	R	S	T	U	V	W	X	Y	Z
21	19	17	6	20	15	3	12	13	9	23	18	8

16 4 11 22 15   16 12 11 22   16 4 13 7 16   5 15

16 7 7 17   5 15   16 4 11 22 15   16 19 2

16 4 13 7 16

Extra page in case you want to practice some more!

Use cursive and write who is your favorite movie character. Use at least 5 words beginning with the letter „D" in your text...

...and draw a funny illustration!

Trace and write the letters:

Now let's try to put some letters together!

ei ei ei

er er er

em em em

ee ee ee

Time for short words - let's dive in!

Easy Easy Easy

Earn Earn Earn

Eat Eat Eat

ear ear ear

end end end

egg egg egg

eye eye eye

My younger brother is dyslexic. The teacher suggested he practice writing, and since he's been practicing cursive writing, his studies and tests are going better! (Oliver, age 12)

Trace these funny sentences and then write them on your own!

Eearnest excited eagle exits
elegant entry.

Eearnest excited eagle exits
elegant entry.

Entire earth enjoys
enchanting emptiness.

Entire earth enjoys
enchanting emptiness.

Trace these jokes and then write them on your own:

What do sprinters eat before a race? Nothing, they fast!

What do

What do duck's tail feathers do? Cover their butt-quacks.

What do

Use your super creativity and write a one-sentence short story using the word „EVERYWHEN"*.

_____

- -

_____

- -

_____

- -

_____

- -

_____

- -

_____

- -

*EVERYWHEN is a word that is very rarely used as an unusual way to say "always" or "all the time."

Solve this puzzle and say it out loud!

A	B	C	D	E	F	G	H	I	J	K	L	M
17	7	15	14	4	16	24	22	18	9	11	19	25

N	O	P	Q	R	S	T	U	V	W	X	Y	Z
13	10	12	21	5	23	20	26	6	2	8	3	1

4 19 4 6 4 13   7 4 13 4 6 10 19 4 13 20

4 19 4 12 22 17 13 20 23

Extra page in case you want to practice some more!

Use cursive and write what makes you special and unique. Use at least 5 words beginning with the letter „E" in your text...

...and draw a funny illustration!

Trace and write the letters:

Now let's try to put some letters together!

fm *fm* *fm*

fc *fc* *fc*

ft *ft* *ft*

fo *fo* *fo*

Time for short words – let's dive in!

Fox *Fox* *Fox*

Fair *Fair* *Fair*

Fact *Fact* *Fact*

far *far* *far*

fill *fill* *fill*

feel *feel* *feel*

face *face* *face*

Writing in cursive made it easier for me to read and understand historical documents on a school trip to the museum, and that impressed my favorite teacher! (Helen, age 8)

Trace these funny sentences and then write them on your own!

Funny friendly ferret faces fascinating fear.

Funny friendly ferret faces fascinating fear.

Fluffy fat flamingo finds fabulous fuchsia figs.

Fluffy fat flamingo finds fabulous fuchsia figs.

Trace these jokes and then write them on your own:

What is harder to catch
the faster you run? Your
breath!

What is

What falls but never gets
hurt? Snow.

What

A graphologist analyzes handwriting and studies the relationship between its character, personality traits, and emotions. They do not require knowledge of a particular language (such as German or Japanese) when analyzing handwritten text. Similarly, they can analyze a psychological profile based on a picture or drawing by a specific author.

Use your super creativity and write a one-sentence short story using the word „FINIFUGAL"*.

_____

- -

_____

- -

_____

- -

_____

- -

_____

- -

_____

- -

_____

- -

_____

*FINIFUGAL - you are finifugal if you're afraid of finishing something, you hate endings; it describes someone who tries to avoid or prolong the final moment of a story, relationship, or some other journey.

Solve this puzzle and say it out loud!

A	B	C	D	E	F	G	H	I	J	K	L	M
16	23	13	25	1	4	19	14	3	12	21	6	10

N	O	P	Q	R	S	T	U	V	W	X	Y	Z
24	7	5	18	17	15	8	26	11	20	9	2	22

4 7 26 17   4 3 24 1   4 17 1 15 14

4 3 15 14   4 7 17   2 7 26

Extra page in case you want to practice some more!

Use cursive and write what you find annoying. Use at least 5 words beginning with the letter „F" in your text...

...and draw a funny illustration!

Trace and write the letters:

Now let's try to put some letters together!

gu *gu* *gu*

gh *gh* *gh*

gr *gr* *gr*

gt *gt* *gt*

Time for short words - let's dive in!

Gun *Gun* *Gun*

Goat *Goat* *Goat*

Girl *Girl* *Girl*

go *go* *go*

gem *gem* *gem*

gear *gear* *gear*

game *game* *game*

I wanted to thank my teacher for helping me with my math homework, and wri-ting the note in cursive made me feel that it was more special! (William, age 9)

The uppercase letter „G" can be also written in this way:

And another version of short words:

Gun *Gun Gun*

Goat *Goat Goat*

Girl *Girl Girl*

Gift *Gift Gift*

Go *Go Go*

Gem *Gem Gem*

Gear *Gear Gear*

Game *Game Game*

Gum *Gum Gum*

Gap *Gap Gap*

Writing with fountain pens turns out to have only advantages. An experiment was conducted in one of the schools in Edinburgh, and it turned out that students who use fountain pens cope better with learning, write more carefully, and in addition, gain higher self-esteem.

Trace these funny sentences and then write them on your own!

Goofy glamorous goats got green glitter.

Greasy gecko grabs gorgeous golden grapes.

Trace these jokes and then write them on your own:

What kind of cars do cooks drive? Chef-rolets.

What

Why didn't the dog want to play football? It was a boxer!

Why

Use your super creativity and write a one-sentence short story using the word „GIBBERISH"*.

*GIBBERISH means nonsense sounds or writing. An example of gibberish is a baby's babble. To gibber or to jabber is to talk rapidly and excitedly without making any sense.

Solve this puzzle and say it out loud!

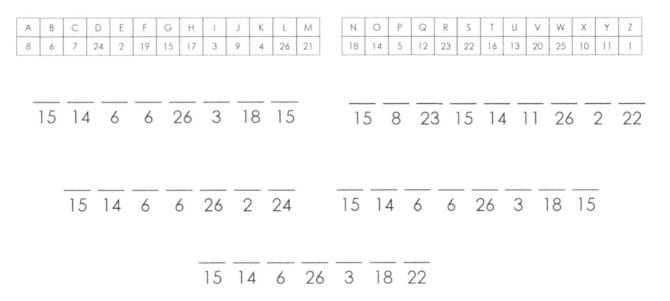

A	B	C	D	E	F	G	H	I	J	K	L	M
8	6	7	24	2	19	15	17	3	9	4	26	21

N	O	P	Q	R	S	T	U	V	W	X	Y	Z
18	14	5	12	23	22	16	13	20	25	10	11	1

15 14 6 6 26 3 18 15

15 8 23 15 14 11 26 2 22

15 14 6 6 26 2 24

15 14 6 6 26 3 18 15

15 14 6 26 3 18 22

Extra page in case you want to practice some more!

You just ate a cookie that turned you 25 feet tall. What do you do next? Use cursive and at least 5 words beginning with the letter „G" in your text...

...and draw a funny illustration!

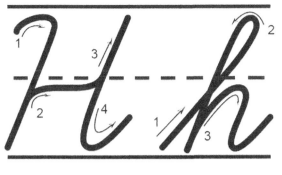

Trace and write the letters:

H H H H H H H H H H H H H

H H H

H

h h h h h h h h h h h h h

h h h

h

Now let's try to put some letters together!

Hn Hn Hn

Hi Hi Hi

Hi Hi Hi

he *he he*

ho *ho ho*

hr *hr hr*

hy *hy hy*

Time for short words - let's dive in!

Hug *Hug Hug*

Hole *Hole Hole*

Help *Help Help*

hot *hot hot*

hill *hill hill*

hat *hat hat*

hop *hop hop*

I managed to create a personalized and unique birthday card for my best friend using cursive. I added some stickers and some glitter and the effect was really great! (Isabella, age 9)

Trace these funny sentences and then write them on your own!

Happy and hungry
hamster holds huge ham.

Happy and hungry
hamster holds huge ham.

Hairy handsome hare has
healthy hazelnuts.

Hairy handsome hare has
healthy hazelnuts.

Trace these jokes and then write them on your own:

What is the parrot's favorite game? Hide and speak.

What is

What do we call a monster that hibernates all winter? Werewolf.

What do

The oldest existing texts are written in the Sumerian language. It was spoken in southern Mesopotamia for at least 4 millennia before our era. Around 2000 BCE, it was replaced in speech by the Akkadian language, but it was still used for ceremonial, literary, and scientific writings until the 1st century CE. Although it was later forgotten, a large number of preserved texts allowed it to be reconstructed. Today, scientists know its vocabulary, grammar, and even the functioning dialects and pronunciation.

Use your super creativity and write a one-sentence short story using the word „HULLABALLOO"*.

*HULLABALLOO is an uproar or a noisy commotion, especially the sound of a bunch of people shouting in protest about something. It doesn't have to be literally noisy. „Hullaballoo" can also be used to name all the talk and commentary surrounding a controversy, such as on social media.

Solve this puzzle and say it out loud!

A	B	C	D	E	F	G	H	I	J	K	L	M
13	20	8	18	15	19	2	25	3	14	7	11	24

N	O	P	Q	R	S	T	U	V	W	X	Y	Z
23	5	16	22	4	17	1	9	10	12	6	21	26

25 13 4 4 21   1 25 15   25 9 23 2 4 21

25 9 23 2 4 21   25 3 16 16 5   3 17

25 13 16 16 3 11 21   15 13 1 3 23 2   25 13 24

Extra page in case you want to practice some more!

Use cursive and write what kind of gifts you like the most. Use at least 5 words beginning with the letter „H" in your text...

...and draw a funny illustration!

Trace and write the letters:

$\mathcal{I}$ l l l l l l l l l l l l l l l

$\mathcal{I}$ l l

$\mathcal{I}$

i i i i i i i i i i i i i i i i i i i

i i i

i

Now let's try to put some letters together!

In In In

Ii Ii Ii

Is Is Is

ik *ik ik*

io *io io*

ir *ir ir*

iw *iw iw*

Time for short words – let's dive in!

Ice *Ice Ice*

Iron *Iron Iron*

Ink *Ink Ink*

ire *ire ire*

ill *ill ill*

idle *idle idle*

ivy *ivy ivy*

We played treasure hunters and I was paired with my friend! We left each other secret messages written in cursive, and no one else could read them! It was great! (Michael, age 10)

Trace these funny sentences and then write them on your own!

Intelligent iguana is inside impressive icy igloo.

Intelligent iguana is inside impressive icy igloo.

Internet is insanely interesting innovation.

Internet is insanely interesting innovation.

Trace these jokes and then write them on your own:

What is a ghost's favorite drink? Ghost-ade.

What is

What room has no doors or windows? Mushroom.

What

Gutenberg invented printing, but it brought him... bankruptcy! The improvement and successful construction of a printing press, as well as the ambitious project of publishing a two-volume Bible, cost Gutenberg a total of 20,000 guilders in loans. The debt led to a lawsuit, bankruptcy, and the loss of his workshop.

Use your super creativity and write a one-sentence short story using the word „INKLE"*.

_____

- -

_____

_____

- -

_____

_____

- -

_____

_____

- -

_____

*INKLE is a colored linen tape or braid woven through a narrow loom.

Solve this puzzle and say it out loud!

A	B	C	D	E	F	G	H	I	J	K	L	M
4	14	9	16	10	1	13	5	19	15	25	23	2

N	O	P	Q	R	S	T	U	V	W	X	Y	Z
26	6	7	8	20	18	12	22	11	17	21	3	24

19   10 4 12   10 10 23   17 5 19 23 10

3 6 22   7 10 10 23   10 10 23

Extra page in case you want to practice some more!

If you had a superpower it would be... Use cursive and at least 5 words beginning with the letter „I" in your text...

...and draw a funny illustration!

Trace and write the letters:

Now let's try to put some letters together!

ja *ja* *ja*

ji *ji* *ji*

jy *jy* *jy*

jh *jh* *jh*

Time for short words - let's dive in!

Jam *Jam* *Jam*

Jade *Jade* *Jade*

Join *Join* *Join*

just *just* *just*

june *june* *june*

joke *joke* *joke*

joy *joy* *joy*

I love using cursive when writing letters because it made them look more formal and special. I write in cursive to my pen friend and she does the same! (Samantha, age 10)

Trace these funny sentences and then write them on your own!

Just jump joyfully jazzy,

jelly jaguar!

Jolly Jeff just jiggles

juicy Jalapeno jam.

Trace these jokes and then write them on your own:

How does a hurricane see?

With one eye.

How does

Why was the math book

sad? Because it had too

many problems.

Why was

Use your super creativity and write a one-sentence short story using the word „JACKANAPES"*.

_____

- -

_____

- -

_____

- -

_____

- -

_____

- -

_____

- -

_____

- -

_____

*JACKANAPES is from the fifteenth century, and it's thought to come from the phrase „Jack of Naples," or to have some connection to the word apes. It's an old fashioned way to describe a cheeky or impertinent person, especially a young man. Your great-grandfather might shake his cane and yell, „Get off my lawn, you jackanapes!" when the neighbor kids lose their basketball in his yard.

Solve this puzzle and say it out loud!

A	B	C	D	E	F	G	H	I	J	K	L	M
7	8	3	4	14	19	10	15	22	16	24	23	6

N	O	P	Q	R	S	T	U	V	W	X	Y	Z
9	20	12	25	5	2	1	11	17	13	18	21	26

16 11 2 1 22 9   16 11 6 12 22 9 10

16 20 21 20 11 2   16 20 22 9 14 4   22 9

16 20 15 9 9 7 2   16 11 8 22 23 14 14

Extra page in case you want to practice some more!

You are the teacher for the day. What will you do in your lesson? Use cursive and at least 5 words beginning with the letter „J" in your text...

...and draw a funny illustration!

Trace and write the letters:

K KKKKKKKKKK

K KK

K

k kkkkkkkkkkkkkk

k kk

k

Now let's try to put some letters together!

Kn Kn Kn

Ko Ko Ko

Kr Kr Kr

ki *ki ki*

ka *ka ka*

ky *ky ky*

ku *ku ku*

Time for short words - let's dive in!

Keg *Keg Keg*

Kept *Kept Kept*

Keen *Keen Keen*

kite *kite kite*

kiss *kiss kiss*

knot *knot knot*

king *king king*

I love to draw and calligraphy, so writing in cursive is also something like art for me. Inspirational words or quotes written in cursive look super professional! (Benjamin, age 12)

Trace these funny sentences and then write them on your own!

Kids kindly kick knitted,
kinesthetic kiwi.

Kids kindly kick knitted,
kinesthetic kiwi.

Knight kidnapped and
kicked koala's kidney.

Knight kidnapped and
kicked koala's kidney.

Trace these jokes and then write them on your own:

What kind of eggs do monsters like? Terri-fried!

What

What do you call a cat who plays the guitar? A furrocious musician

What do

In 1938, Hungarian journalist Laszlo Biro presented the world with a prototype of the ballpoint pen we know today. He improved on the technology of the ballpoint pen invented in the United States. The ink used in the pen smeared and spread, making it difficult to work with. Biro, who had already noticed that printing ink dried much faster and did not smear, prepared an ink with properties that combined both ink and paint with the help of his chemist brother. They also incorporated the ball mechanism from the pen design, which worked well for regulating ink flow in the pen.

Use your super creativity and write a one-sentence short story using the word „KIBITZER"*.

*KIBITZER is a Yiddish word and is a synonym for a backseat driver. It can describe a person who is eager to give advice about something for which they are not responsible.

Solve this puzzle and say it out loud!

A	B	C	D	E	F	G	H	I	J	K	L	M
21	15	24	9	1	25	26	10	5	17	11	6	20

N	O	P	Q	R	S	T	U	V	W	X	Y	Z
7	3	16	22	4	19	18	2	14	8	23	13	12

11 1 7 7 13   5 19   5 7   18 10 1

11 5 18 24 10 1 7   1 21 18 5 7 26

11 5 18 11 21 18

Extra page in case you want to practice some more!

Use cursive and write what if cows could drive cars. Use at least 5 words beginning with the letter „K" in your text...

...and draw a funny illustration!

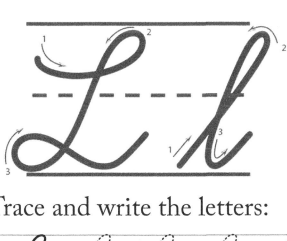

Trace and write the letters:

Now let's try to put some letters together!

le *le* *le*

lm *lm* *lm*

lk *lk* *lk*

ll *ll* *ll*

Time for short words - let's dive in!

Lock *Lock* *Lock*

Lyre *Lyre* *Lyre*

Lid *Lid* *Lid*

lolly *lolly* *lolly*

low *low* *low*

lion *lion* *lion*

love *love* *love*

My older sister says that her professor talked about studies that proved that practicing writing helps later in learning, remembering and processing information. Sounds great and has encouraged me to keep practicing! (Anya, age 11)

Trace these funny sentences and then write them on your own!

Lovely lady llama likes lonely laziness.

Loyal lemur loves lustrous lime lettuce.

Trace these jokes and then write them on your own:

What is an astronaut's

favorite drink? Gravi-tea.

What is

What do we call the cros-

sing of a cat and a lemon?

A sourpuss.

What do

Kubotan is a self-defense tool. It is a 14-centimeter rod carried as a keychain. It is designed for striking and pressing certain points on the body, such as the face, neck, larynx, nerve plexuses, or joints. It can also be used to strike bones. One type of kubotan is a tactical pen, which is a pen with additional functions. It is primarily disguised. Only people familiar with the topic will realize that we are not using an ordinary pen, but a self-defense accessory.

Use your super creativity and write a one-sentence short story using the word „LOLLYGAG"*.

_____

_____

_____

_____

_____

_____

_____

_____

_____

_____

_____

*LOLLYGAG describes someone who is messing around and doing something that isn't useful.
For example: He goes to the beach to lollygag in the sun.

Solve this puzzle and say it out loud!

A	B	C	D	E	F	G	H	I	J	K	L	M	N	O	P	Q	R	S	T	U	V	W	X	Y	Z
6	4	16	24	12	14	20	15	17	7	21	1	11	3	18	2	26	23	5	9	8	13	10	22	19	25

— — — — —   — — — —   — — —
1 6 23 23 19   5 12 3 9   9 15 12

— — — — — —   —   — — — — — —
1 6 9 9 12 23   6   1 12 9 9 12 23

— — — — —
1 6 9 12 23

Extra page in case you want to practice some more!

It started out just like an ordinary day, but then... Use cursive and at least 5 words beginning with the letter „L" in your text...

...and draw a funny illustration!

Mm

Trace and write the letters:

M M M M M M M M M M

M M M

M

m m m m m m m m m

m m m

m

Now let's try to put some letters together!

Mi Mi Mi

Ms Ms Ms

Mr Mr Mr

me *me me*

mk *mk mk*

mc *mc mc*

ma *ma ma*

Time for short words - let's dive in!

Mom *Mom Mom*

Mail *Mail Mail*

Mud *Mud Mud*

man *man man*

mole *mole mole*

moo *moo moo*

mat *mat mat*

I got a travel journal for my birthday and I want my journals to look cool, so I'm learning to write in cursive. (Sebastian, age 7)

The uppercase letter „M" can be also written in this way:

M M M

M M M

M M M

M

M

Mo Mo Mo

Ms Ms Ms

Ml Ml Ml

Mu Mu Mu

Me Me Me

Mi Mi Mi

Mr Mr Mr

And another version of short words:

Mom *Mom* *Mom*

Mail *Mail* *Mail*

Mud *Mud* *Mud*

Mist *Mist* *Mist*

Man *Man* *Man*

Mole *Mole* *Mole*

Mid *Mid* *Mid*

Milk *Milk* *Milk*

Mug *Mug* *Mug*

Scientists have proven that handwriting activates more areas of the brain than typing on a computer, tablet, or smartphone. Among the participants in the experiment, after an hour of taking notes, those who wrote by hand remembered more than those who used electronic devices. Volunteers who wrote by hand not only remembered better but also took notes faster compared to those who wrote on tablets or smartphones, even when special pens were used on tablets. Scientists are convinced that handwriting can also support creative thinking. Therefore, the study's authors encourage not to abandon writing on paper.

Trace these funny sentences and then write them on your own!

Mother mouse makes
marshmallow macaroni.

Mother mouse makes
marshmallow macaroni.

Muttering mammoth
Mark makes mortgages.

Muttering mammoth
Mark makes mortgages.

Trace these jokes and then write them on your own:

What fruit do scarecrows love the most?

Straw-berries.

What

What is the best thing to put into a pie? Your teeth.

What is

The most expensive pen is the Heaven Gold - it cost one million dollars and was created by Anita Tan. It is made of 24-carat pink gold and adorned with 1888 diamonds weighing 48 carats. 161 of the diamonds have fancy colors, giving the pen a unique character.

Use your super creativity and write a one-sentence short story using the word „MACARONIC"*.

_____

_____

_____

_____

_____

----

*MACARONIC refers to when someone mixes two different languages together. Especially when someone mixes vernacular words with Latin words or non-Latin words with Latin endings. You can use it also to describe things like this: my drawer is a macaronic hodgepodge of unmatched socks.

Solve this puzzle and say it out loud!

A	B	C	D	E	F	G	H	I	J	K	L	M
18	24	26	13	22	10	11	16	9	21	8	23	4

N	O	P	Q	R	S	T	U	V	W	X	Y	Z
17	12	6	3	25	5	15	20	19	7	14	2	1

4 9 11 16 15 2   4 9 8 22   4 18 8 22 5

4 18 25 19 22 23 23 12 20 5   4 20 17 26 16 9 22 5

10 12 25   4 18 25 2

Extra page in case you want to practice some more!

Use cursive and write what food can you not live without? Why?
Use at least 5 words beginning with the letter „M" in your text...

...and draw a funny illustration!

Trace and write the letters:

n n n n n n n n n n

n n n

n

m m m m m m m m m m m

m m m

m

Now let's try to put some letters together!

Ne Ne Ne

Ni Ni Ni

Ny Ny Ny

no *no no*

na *na na*

mu *mu mu*

nh *nh nh*

Time for short words – let's dive in!

New *New New*

Nine *Nine Nine*

Ninja *Ninja Ninja*

nap *nap nap*

next *next next*

nail *nail nail*

neck *neck neck*

I got a beautiful leather notebook for my birthday! It's very vintage and I write my diary in it. I want it to be unique inside too, so I try to write it in cursive and it looks like out of an old movie. He is like a friend to whom I can confide any secret! (Parker, age 9)

Trace these funny sentences and then write them on your own!

Nine nice, nifty minis
need neon, meat napkins
Nine nice, nifty minis
need neon, meat napkins

Noisy narwhal Ned
nagged noble nutria.
Noisy narwhal Ned
nagged noble nutria.

Trace these jokes and then write them on your own:

Why don't oysters give to charity? They're shellfish.

Why

Which part of the deck stinks the most? The poop deck.

Which

The caps of pens have holes. They were introduced because of the large number of deaths due to choking on pen caps - about 100 people per year.

Use your super creativity and write a one-sentence short story using the word „NOOB"*.

---

*NOOB is word that we use when we describe someone who is inexperienced at something, usually in relation to using the internet or playing a video game.

Solve this puzzle and say it out loud!

A	B	C	D	E	F	G	H	I	J	K	L	M	N	O	P	Q	R	S	T	U	V	W	X	Y	Z
15	6	7	9	2	1	24	5	25	14	10	16	8	17	20	22	4	11	19	3	26	12	13	21	18	23

17 25 17 2   17 25 8 6 16 2   17 20 6 16 2 8 2 17

17 25 6 6 16 2 9   17 12 3 19

Extra page in case you want to practice some more!

Use cursive and describe the oldest person you know? Use at least 5 words beginning with the letter „N" in your text...

...and draw a funny illustration!

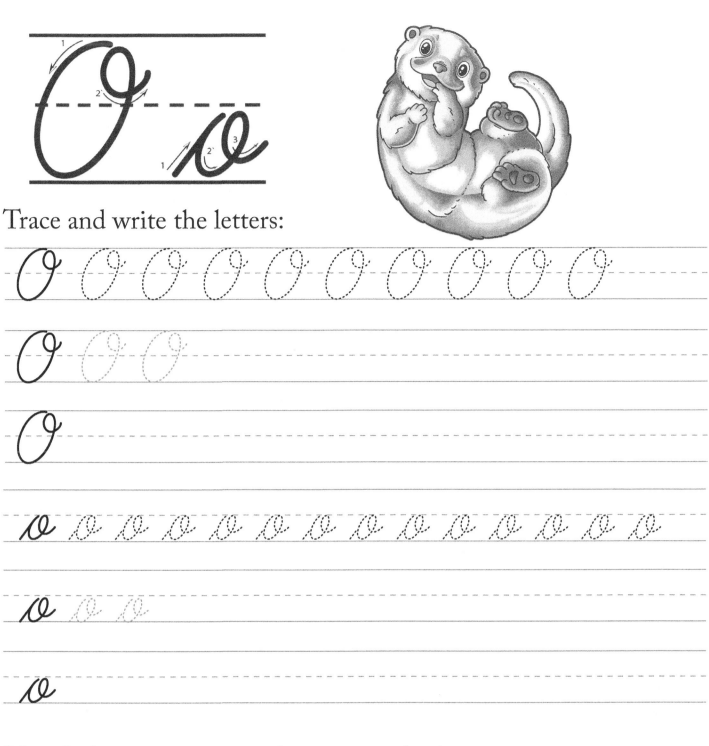

Trace and write the letters:

Now let's try to put some letters together!

on no no

od od od

oh oh oh

ok ok ok

Time for short words - let's dive in!

Our Our Our

Old Old Old

Off Off Off

one one one

owl owl owl

oil oil oil

odd odd odd

My family went to a fancy restaurant and I could read the menu written in cursive so I could choose my meal myself. My parents were impressed! (Colton, age 8)

Trace these funny sentences and then write them on your own!

Outgoing otters obsessed with original oatmeal.

Odd optimistic owl in orange onsie orders olives.

Trace these jokes and then write them on your own:

Why don't ants get sick?

They have tiny ant-bodies.

Why

What do you call a computer superhero?

A Screen Saver!

What do

Pens created for astronauts have special properties. They work underwater, in a vacuum and on oily surfaces, and additionally last three times longer than regular pens.

Use your super creativity and write a one-sentence short story using the word „OXTER"*.

*OXTER is just an outdated term for "armpit."

Solve this puzzle and say it out loud!

A	B	C	D	E	F	G	H	I	J	K	L	M
23	18	3	13	2	4	21	25	1	6	10	5	7

N	O	P	Q	R	S	T	U	V	W	X	Y	Z
16	11	12	9	22	15	26	24	14	17	20	19	8

11 13 13   11 5 13   11 5 5 1 2

11 1 5 15   11 1 5 19   23 24 26 11 15

Extra page in case you want to practice some more!

You have $1000 to spend. What will you buy? Use at least 5 words beginning with the letter „O" in your text...

...and draw a funny illustration!

Trace and write the letters:

$\mathcal{P}$ $\mathcal{P}$ $\mathcal{P}$ $\mathcal{P}$ $\mathcal{P}$ $\mathcal{P}$ $\mathcal{P}$ $\mathcal{P}$ $\mathcal{P}$ $\mathcal{P}$ $\mathcal{P}$ $\mathcal{P}$ $\mathcal{P}$

$\mathcal{P}$ $\mathcal{P}$ $\mathcal{P}$

$\mathcal{P}$

p p p p p p p p p p p p p

p p p p

p

Now let's try to put some letters together!

$\mathcal{P}o$ $\mathcal{P}o$ $\mathcal{P}o$

$\mathcal{P}l$ $\mathcal{P}l$ $\mathcal{P}l$

$\mathcal{P}i$ $\mathcal{P}i$ $\mathcal{P}i$

pr *pr* *pr*

ps *ps* *ps*

pm *pm* *pm*

pp *pp* *pp*

Time for short words - let's dive in!

Past *Past* *Past*

Pie *Pie* *Pie*

Pen *Pen* *Pen*

post *post* *post*

play *play*

pad *pad* *pad*

pet *pet* *pet*

I'm always so excited to sign permission slips in cursive because it felt like a real signature, like the ones I saw on important documents. (Summer, age 8)

Trace these funny sentences and then write them on your own!

Poor plan – poor perfor-

mance.

Pretty powerful parrot

pushed prudent princess.

Trace these jokes and then write them on your own:

How do trees usually get on the Internet? They log in!

How do

What do you call a bear with no teeth? A gummy bear.

What do

The English language is a native language for over 527 million people. It is learned by over 1.5 billion people worldwide and is an official language in 67 countries around the world.

Use your super creativity and write a one-sentence short story using the word „POPPLE"*.

_____

- -

_____

_____

- -

_____

_____

- -

_____

_____

- -

_____

*Popple as a noun it means boilng water or choppy sea. As a verb - to flow in a tumbling or very rippling way, like „you could hear the sound of the water poppling and splashing".

Solve this puzzle and say it out loud!

A	B	C	D	E	F	G	H	I	J	K	L	M
12	18	2	20	15	5	21	17	22	14	8	25	3

N	O	P	Q	R	S	T	U	V	W	X	Y	Z
16	6	26	4	24	13	19	11	10	9	23	1	7

26 15 19 15 24   26 22 26 15 24   26 22 2 8 15 20

12   26 15 2 8   6 5   26 22 2 8 25 15 20

26 15 26 26 15 24 13

Extra page in case you want to practice some more!

Use cursive and describe your ideal birthday cake Use at least 5 words beginning with the letter „P" in your text...

...and draw a funny illustration!

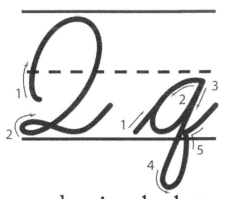

Trace and write the letters:

Q Q Q Q Q Q Q Q Q Q Q Q Q

Q Q Q

Q

q q q q q q q q q q q q q

q q q

q

Now let's try to put some letters together!

Qn Qn Qn

Qu Qu Qu

Qa Qa Qa

qe qe qe

qu qu qu

qc qc qc

ql ql ql

Time for short words - let's dive in!

Quack Quack Quack

Quote Quote Quote

Quick Quick Quick

quit quit quit

quad quad quad

quiz quiz quiz

quiet quiet quiet

I created a handmade gift for my friend and included a handmade card. It was supposed to be in a vintage style, so it was very useful for me that I can write in cursive. It turned out great and my friend was impressed! (Axel, age 12)

Trace these funny sentences and then write them on your own!

Quirky qualified queen
quits quiet quilting.

Quokkas quarter quickly
quaintly quacks quotes.

Trace these jokes and then write them on your own:

What do you call a baby owl? An owlet.

What do

Why did the grape stop in the middle of the road? It ran out of juice.

Why did

Even the ancient Egyptians used reed „pens" for writing on papyrus. Predecessors to modern pens, now rarely used, included bird feathers, reed pens, fountain pens, and brushes.

Use your super creativity and write a one-sentence short story using the word „QUAB"*.

_____

_____

_____

_____

_____

_____

*QUAB means an unfledged bird, something immature or unfinished.

Solve this puzzle and say it out loud!

A	B	C	D	E	F	G	H	I	J	K	L	M	N	O	P	Q	R	S	T	U	V	W	X	Y	Z
4	6	22	11	25	7	15	13	12	14	10	3	2	1	19	5	26	18	20	23	21	8	17	24	9	16

23 13 25   26 21 25 25 1   22 19 12 1 25 11

26 21 12 22 10   22 3 12 5 5 25 11

26 21 12 5 20

Extra page in case you want to practice some more!

Finish the story: When I'm older I want to be an expert in... Use cursive and at least 5 words beginning with the letter „Q" in your text...

...and draw a funny illustration!

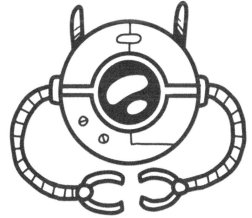

Trace and write the letters:

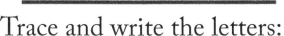

R R R R R R R R R R

R R R

R

n n n n n n n n n n n n n n n n n n

n n n n n

n

Now let's try to put some letters together!

Re Re Re

Ry Ry Ry

Rd Rd Rd

rg *rg* *rg*

rh *rh* *rh*

ra *ra* *ra*

ru *ru* *ru*

Time for short words - let's dive in!

Roll *Roll* *Roll*

Rice *Rice* *Rice*

Race *Race* *Race*

rug *rug* *rug*

rare *rare* *rare*

run *run* *run*

rock *rock* *rock*

I love creating stories and writing stories. Someday I'd like to write my own book! Since I've
been writing in cursive, I've noticed that my stories are better and I write them faster. I don't
focus on every letter, I just write what's on my mind! (Madison, age 11)

Trace these funny sentences and then write them on your own!

Red, robust, reliable rab-
bits run really rapidly.

Ripe, reverent, rural roses
rarely reservedly reek.

Trace these jokes and then write them on your own:

What do you call a deer
with no eyes? No idea.

What do

Does mummy enjoy being
mummy? Of corpse!

Does

The Morse code was named after the inventor of the telegraph - Samuel Morse. It is an international code consisting of 26 letters from A to Z. There is no differentiation between upper and lower case letters in this notation. The most commonly used distress signal is SOS (three dots, three dashes, and three dots). It is used all over the world. The SOS signal was first used by the German naval infantry in 1904. The duration of a dash is equivalent to that of three dots.

Use your super creativity and write a one-sentence short story using the word „RATOON"*.

_____

_____

_____

_____

_____

_____

_____

_____

_____

_____

_____

_____

*RATOON is a tiny shoot that sprouts from a plant, especially during the springtime.

Solve this puzzle and say it out loud!

A	B	C	D	E	F	G	H	I	J	K	L	M	N	O	P	Q	R	S	T	U	V	W	X	Y	Z
5	21	7	26	24	1	11	25	17	2	19	20	23	8	3	22	15	10	14	16	12	4	13	6	18	9

10 3 10 18 14   20 5 13 8   10 5 19 24

10 5 10 24 20 18   10 5 19 24 14

10 24 5 20 20 18   10 17 11 25 16

Extra page in case you want to practice some more!

A courier has just delivered you a mysterious box. What's inside? Use cursive and at least 5 words beginning with the letter „R" in your text...

...and draw a funny illustration!

Trace and write the letters:

Now let's try to put some letters together!

sa *sa sa*

sd *sd sd*

sg *sg sg*

si *si si*

Time for short words - let's dive in!

Sad *Sad Sad*

Sky *Sky Sky*

Six *Six Six*

salt *salt salt*

star *star star*

sun *sun sun*

silk *silk silk*

I wrote a poem in cursive for my mom on Mother's Day, and she cried tears of joy!
(Brayden, age 9)

Trace these funny sentences and then write them on your own!

Sweet, stylish Sally sings
sad sassy songs.

Sweet, stylish Sally sings
sad sassy songs.

Skilled Sam slapped
Simon's shiny scalp.

Skilled Sam slapped
Simon's shiny scalp.

Trace these jokes and then write them on your own:

What is red and bad for your teeth? A brick.

What is

What does baby corn say to momma corn? Where is the popcorn?

What does

In 1949, Marcel Bich created the first ballpoint pen available to the mass market. He named it „Bic" after his own surname. An average BIC pen can draw a continuous line that is 2 kilometers long.

Use your super creativity and write a one-sentence short story using the word „**SKIRL**"*.

_____

- -

_____

_____

- -

_____

_____

- -

_____

_____

- -

_____

*SKIRL is just an outdated term for "armpit."

Solve this puzzle and say it out loud!

A	B	C	D	E	F	G	H	I	J	K	L	M	N	O	P	Q	R	S	T	U	V	W	X	Y	Z
1	25	20	19	6	11	12	17	21	8	10	5	7	15	24	3	16	23	22	18	9	26	13	4	2	14

22 21 4   22 21 20 10   17 21 20 10 22

15 21 20 10 22   22 21 4   22 5 21 20 10

25 23 21 20 10 22   13 21 18 17   3 21 20 10 22

Extra page in case you want to practice some more!

Use cursive and write a short story about a snow day. Use at least 5 words beginning with the letter „S" in your text...

...and draw a funny illustration!

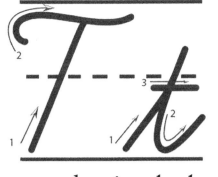

Trace and write the letters:

T T T T T T T T T T T T T T

T T T

T

t t t t t t t t t t t t t t

t t t t t

t

Now let's try to put some letters together!

Tn Tn Tn

Tr Tr Tr

Ts Ts Ts

tm *tm tm*

to *to to*

tl *tl tl*

tt *tt tt*

Time for short words – let's dive in!

Tell *Tell Tell*

Toe *Toe Toe*

Top *Top Top*

tea *tea tea*

tall *tall tall*

tan *tan tan*

tip *tip tip*

I used to hate reading because it felt like a chore. But once I learned cursive, I noticed that I was able to read faster and more fluently. Now reading is much easier and quicker! (Amy, age 8)

Trace these funny sentences and then write them on your own!

Teal turtles travelled tire-
lessly through the tundra.

Teal turtles travelled tire-
lessly through the tundra.

Tender tigers thanked their
tall, tenacious, teachers.

Tender tigers thanked their
tall, tenacious, teachers.

Trace these jokes and then write them on your own:

Where do pencils come from? Pennsylvania.

Where do

How do clams call the in friends? On their shell phones!

How do

Use your super creativity and write a one-sentence short story using the word „TARADIDDLE"*.

_____
- -
_____
- -
_____
- -
_____
- -
_____
- -
_____
- -
_____
- -
_____

*TARADIDDLE is used when you want to explain that something someone is talking about is a childlish lie, over-exaggerated or pretentious nonsense. For example: „Yesterday she told me taradiddle about having ‚working quite a lot'".

Solve this puzzle and say it out loud!

A	B	C	D	E	F	G	H	I	J	K	L	M
4	24	17	8	9	15	26	6	7	22	25	14	19

N	O	P	Q	R	S	T	U	V	W	X	Y	Z
18	1	12	13	16	11	5	3	10	2	23	20	21

5 9 18   5 4 19 9   5 4 8 12 1 14 9 11

5 3 17 25 9 8   5 7 26 6 5 14 20

5 1 26 9 5 6 9 16   7 18   4   5 6 7 18

Extra page in case you want to practice some more!

What if you lived in a swimming pool? Use cursive and at least 5 words beginning with the letter „T" in your text...

...and draw a funny illustration!

Trace and write the letters:

U U U U U U U U U U U U U U

U U U

U

u u u u u u u u u u u u u u u u

u u u

u

Now let's try to put some letters together!

Un Un Un

Us Us Us

Up Up Up

um _um_ _um_

uc _uc_ _uc_

uj _uj_ _uj_

uo _uo_ _uo_

Time for short words - let's dive in!

Ups _Ups_ _Ups_

Undo _Undo_ _Undo_

Urge _Urge_ _Urge_

use _use_ _use_

udon _udon_ _udon_

user _user_ _user_

unit _unit_ _unit_

I wrote a thank you note in cursive to my grandparents for a special gift, and they said it
was the nicest thank you they'd ever received. (Philip, age 8)

Trace these funny sentences and then write them on your own!

Urban unicorns use

unique umber umbrellas.

Ugly, unlucky urial is

ultimately upset.

Trace these jokes and then write them on your own:

How does a computer catch a fish? With its internet.

How does

How do clams call their friends? On their shell phones!

How do

Presidents of the United States never use the same pen twice to sign important documents.

Use your super creativity and write a one-sentence short story using the word „UFOLOGY"*.

_____

- -

_____

- -

_____

- -

_____

- -

_____

- -

_____

*UFOLOGY is the study and investigation of UFOs or unidentified flying objects.

Solve this puzzle and say it out loud!

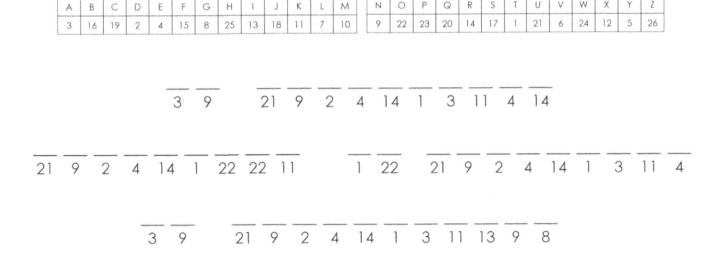

A	B	C	D	E	F	G	H	I	J	K	L	M
3	16	19	2	4	15	8	25	13	18	11	7	10

N	O	P	Q	R	S	T	U	V	W	X	Y	Z
9	22	23	20	14	17	1	21	6	24	12	5	26

3 9   21 9 2 4 14 1 3 11 4 14

21 9 2 4 14 1 22 22 11   1 22   21 9 2 4 14 1 3 11 4

3 9   21 9 2 4 14 1 3 11 13 9 8

Extra page in case you want to practice some more!

What if you could bring any animal to school? Use cursive and at least 5 words beginning with the letter „U" in your text...

...and draw a funny illustration!

Trace and write the letters:

Now let's try to put some letters together!

vi vi vi

ve ve ve

vil vil vil

vj vj vj

Time for short words - let's dive in!

Van Van Van

Video Video Video

Vet Vet Vet

vow vow vow

vibe vibe vibe

very very very

vox vox vox

Cursive helps me focus better on my writing and I like how it looks, it's pretty and fancy.
(Victoria, age 9)

Trace these funny sentences and then write them on your own!

Violet, vigilant vampire visited vast vulcano.

Vesicular, vibrant, vital virus varies violently.

Trace these jokes and then write them on your own:

How did the phone propose
to its love? It gave her a
ring.

How did

What snakes are found on
cars? Windshield wipers.

What

Use your super creativity and write a one-sentence short story using the word „VEXED"*.

_____

_____

_____

_____

_____

_____

_____

*VEXED means that something is difficult and problematic. It also means to be annoyed, frustrated or worried. For example: "I'm very vexed with my cat!".

Solve this puzzle and say it out loud!

A	B	C	D	E	F	G	H	I	J	K	L	M
16	19	3	15	25	24	22	7	26	17	2	5	10

N	O	P	Q	R	S	T	U	V	W	X	Y	Z
4	21	1	9	14	6	23	13	11	8	20	18	12

11 26 4 3 25 4 23   11 21 8 25 15

11 25 4 22 25 16 4 3 25

11 25 14 18   11 25 7 25 10 25 4 23 5 18

Extra page in case you want to practice some more!

If you could add any type of room to your house, what would it be? Use cursive and at least 5 words beginning with the letter „V" in your text...

...and draw a funny illustration!

Trace and write the letters:

Now let's try to put some letters together!

wg wg wg

wh wh wh

wa wa wa

we we we

Time for short words - let's dive in!

Wed Wed Wed

Wee Wee Wee

Wry Wry Wry

why why why

who who who

wet wet wet

wow wow wow

When I visited my grandmother in the nursing home, I could read her old letters and diaries written in cursive. It was amazing, I felt like I was traveling back in time and got to know my grandma so much better! (Max, age 11)

Trace these funny sentences and then write them on your own!

Will witty, wild Will
Wellington win Waterloo?

Will witty, wild Will
Wellington win Waterloo?

Wet, watchful wolves
walk the wrong way.

Wet, watchful wolves
walk the wrong way.

Trace these jokes and then write them on your own:

What did the tree say to the wind? Leaf me alone!

What did

How did the phone propose to its love? It gave her a ring.

How did

Before the Romans introduced the Latin alphabet, the population inhabiting the present-day British Isles used runes for writing, which is a type of alphabet typical for Germanic peoples.

Use your super creativity and write a one-sentence short story using the word „WAMBLE"*.

----

*WAMBLE means an unsteady walk or feeling rumble, nausea of a stomach.

Solve this puzzle and say it out loud!

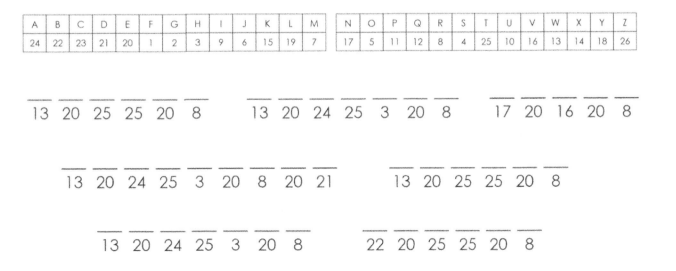

A	B	C	D	E	F	G	H	I	J	K	L	M
24	22	23	21	20	1	2	3	9	15	6	19	7

N	O	P	Q	R	S	T	U	V	W	X	Y	Z
17	5	11	12	8	4	25	10	16	13	14	18	26

13 20 25 25 20 8   13 20 24 25 3 20 8   17 20 16 20 8

13 20 24 25 3 20 8 20 21   13 20 25 25 20 8

13 20 24 25 3 20 8   22 20 25 25 20 8

Extra page in case you want to practice some more!

You get to change the school uniform. What would you make everyone wear and why? Use cursive and at least 5 words beginning with the letter „W" in your text...

...and draw a funny illustration!

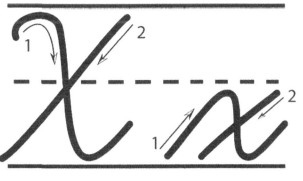 

Trace and write the letters:

$\mathcal{X}$ $\mathcal{X}$ $\mathcal{X}$ $\mathcal{X}$ $\mathcal{X}$ $\mathcal{X}$ $\mathcal{X}$ $\mathcal{X}$ $\mathcal{X}$ $\mathcal{X}$ $\mathcal{X}$

$\mathcal{X}$ $\mathcal{X}$ $\mathcal{X}$

$\mathcal{X}$

x x x x x x x x x x x x

x x x x

x

Now let's try to put some letters together!

$\mathcal{X}e$ $\mathcal{X}e$ $\mathcal{X}e$

$\mathcal{X}d$ $\mathcal{X}d$ $\mathcal{X}d$

$\mathcal{X}i$ $\mathcal{X}i$ $\mathcal{X}i$

xo xo xo

xa xa xa

xj xj xj

xr xr xr

Time for short words - let's dive in!

XOXO XOXO XOXO

XD XD XD

Xenic Xenic Xenic

xxx xxx xxx

x-ray x-ray x-ray

xyst xyst xyst

xerox xerox xerox

Trace these funny sentences and then write them on your own!

Xavier has Xanax and
xenogenic xenophobia.

Xenial xylophonists use
laxative xylitol.

Trace these jokes and then write them on your own:

Why don't zebras play cards in the jungle? Too many cheetahs.

Why

What is the robot's favorite snack? Micro-chips.

What is

English is the official language of airspace. This means that aviation personnel and airport staff must communicate in English. This is why the pilot and crew always speak English fluently, regardless of where they are flying from and to.

Use your super creativity and write a one-sentence short story using the word „XERTZ"*.

_____

- -

_____

- -

_____

- -

_____

- -

_____

- -

*XERTZ is pronounced ‚zerts'. It means to gulp something down quickly and/or in a greedy way'. In most cases, it is used to describe drinking, but it may also describe someone eating quickly. Example sentence: "I was thirsty and I needed to xertz a bottle of water."

Solve this puzzle and say it out loud!

A	B	C	D	E	F	G	H	I	J	K	L	M
6	7	15	19	14	26	13	20	25	10	18	9	8

N	O	P	Q	R	S	T	U	V	W	X	Y	Z
2	1	22	4	16	24	12	23	3	5	21	17	11

21 6 2 19 14 16   14 21 6 8 25 2 14 24

21 17 9 1 22 20 1 2 14 24   5 20 25 9 14

21 14 16 1 21 25 2 13   21 16 6 17 24

Extra page in case you want to practice some more!

What flavor of chips is you favorite and why? Use cursive and at least 5 words beginning with the letter „X" in your text...

...and draw a funny illustration!

Trace and write the letters:

Now let's try to put some letters together!

yo *yo* *yo*

ya *ya* *ya*

ye *ye* *ye*

ym *ym* *ym*

Time for short words - let's dive in!

Yet *Yet* *Yet*

You *You* *You*

Yeti *Yeti* *Yeti*

yes *yes* *yes*

yup *yup* *yup*

yuck *yuck* *yuck*

yoyo *yoyo* *yoyo*

I practiced writing cursive every day, and now I can write faster and
neater! (Connor, age 10)

Trace these funny sentences and then write them on your own!

Young yak yanked
yellow yearlong yacht.

Young yak yanked
yellow yearlong yacht.

Youngster yuppie yawns
and yields yummy yerba.

Youngster yuppie yawns
and yields yummy yerba.

Trace these jokes and then write them on your own:

Where do dogs park their cars? In the banking lot.

Where do

When can you know that a vampire has a cold? He starts coffin.

When can

The English language becomes richer by a new word every two hours. The editors of the popular English-language Oxford English Dictionary have estimated that the English vocabulary increases by around 4,000 new words every year. This means that a new word appears on average every two hours!

Use your super creativity and write a one-sentence short story using the word „YITTEN"*.

---

*YITTEN means frightened in Northern England dialect.

Solve this puzzle and say it out loud!

A	B	C	D	E	F	G	H	I	J	K	L	M
8	7	11	15	13	21	24	5	6	23	17	9	16

N	O	P	Q	R	S	T	U	V	W	X	Y	Z
19	4	10	20	1	14	12	2	3	26	22	25	18

25 4 2 19 24   25 4 9 8 19 15 8   25 8 12 13 14

9 4 3 13 14   25 13 9 9 4 26   25 4 25 4 14

25 4 24 2 1 12   8 19 15

Extra page in case you want to practice some more!

You dig the world's deepest hole. What lies at the bottom? Use cursive and at least 5 words beginning with the letter „Y" in your text...

...and draw a funny illustration!

Trace and write the letters:

Now let's try to put some letters together!

Zz *Zz* *Zz*

za *za* *za*

zo *zo* *zo*

zh *zh* *zh*

Time for short words - let's dive in!

Zoom *Zoom* *Zoom*

Zeal *Zeal* *Zeal*

Zone *Zone* *Zone*

zit *zit* *zit*

zen *zen* *zen*

zoo *zoo* *zoo*

zap *zap* *zap*

Writing in cursive has helped me write faster and more neatly in my schoolwork. I don't
have to lift my pen as much. (Sophie, age 9)

Trace these funny sentences and then write them on your own!

Zippy zombielike zebra zigzags zoo gone.

Zany zoologist has zygomorphic zyst.

Trace these jokes and then write them on your own:

What is the name of a polar bear bank? A snow bank!

What is

What is an insect's favorite sport? Cricket!

What is

A sentence containing all the letters of the alphabet is called a pangram. An example of a well-known English pangram is: „The quick brown fox jumps over a lazy dog."

Use your super creativity and write a one-sentence short story using the word „**ZAZZY**"*.

---

*ZAZZY means shiny or flashy, for example: zazzy shoes.

Solve this puzzle and say it out loud!

A	B	C	D	E	F	G	H	I	J	K	L	M
5	12	19	13	17	4	9	16	26	3	8	15	24

N	O	P	Q	R	S	T	U	V	W	X	Y	Z
2	20	18	21	10	22	11	25	6	7	23	1	14

___ ___ ___ ___ ___ ___
14 26 14 14 26 22

___ ___ ___ ___ ___
14 26 18 18 1

___ ___ ___ ___ ___ ___
14 26 18 18 17 10

___ ___ ___ ___
14 26 18 22

Extra page in case you want to practice some more!

If you could keep any animal as a pet, which one would you choose? Why? Use cursive and at least 5 words beginning with the letter „Z" in your text...

...and draw a funny illustration!

Woooohooo! Isn't that crazy! Look at you!

Now you're a real Master and you can even write a beautiful cursive: "Cursive writing is my new life passion! I love it!" Isn't it beautiful?

Come on, let's have even more fun! Write it down!

And if you want to practice a little more, check out our other books!

Made in the USA
Las Vegas, NV
15 March 2024

87264891R00096